Dog Walks

South Downs - Central

West Sussex

Publishing Ltd

www.countrysidedogwalks.co.uk

First published in November 2014 by **Wet Nose Publishing Ltd**,
Summer Roost
Graigfechan
Denbighshire
LL15 2EU
All enquiries regarding sales telephone: 01824 704398
email cdw@wetnosepublishing.co.uk
www.countrysidedogwalks.co.uk
ISBN 978-0-9573722-9-0

We would like to thank Daisy Gibbs

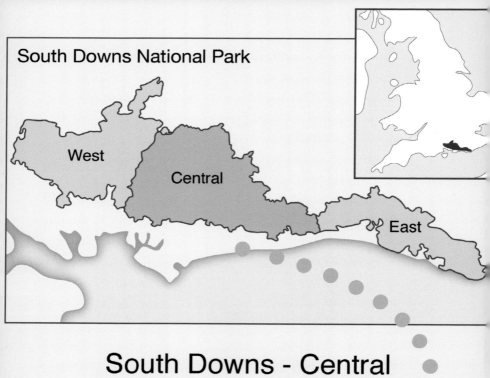

South Downs National Park

West

Central

East

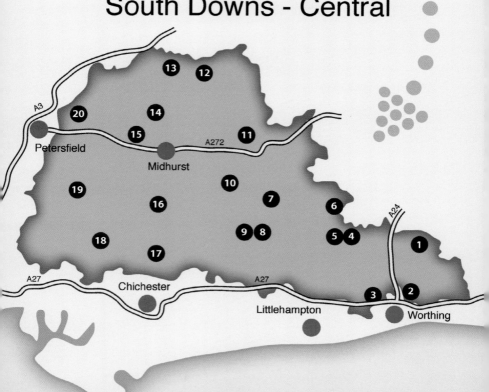

South Downs - Central

A3

20

Petersfield

13

12

14

15

A272

11

Midhurst

19

10

16

7

9 8

6

5 4

A24

1

18

17

A27

Chichester

A27

Littlehampton

3

2

Worthing

Contents

Introduction

The twenty walks included in this book are all designed so that you and your wet nosed friend have a really enjoyable time. Where there are stiles, they are specially designed with lift gates for dogs. At a quick glance there is information at the beginning of each walk to tell you what to expect and what you may need to take with you. The descriptive guides will also warn of any roads ahead or areas of livestock so that you can get your dog on the lead well in advance.

Dogs just love to explore new places. They really enjoy the new smells and carry themselves a little higher with the added excitement. Going to new places gets you and your dog out and about, meeting new people and their dogs. It is important to socialise dogs, as they will be more likely to act in a friendly manner towards other dogs as they gain confidence.

The stunning pictures in this book are just a taster of what you can see along the way. Many of the walks have fantastic views and scenery. Some of the walks are wooded, offering shade on those hot summer days.

The walks are graded Easy, Medium and Challenging. They are all around one to three hours long, depending on your and your dog's pace. You may start with the easy ones and work up to the challenging walks depending on your and your dog's fitness.

Ground Nesting Birds

Watch out for vulnerable ground nesting birds during 1st of March until the end of July. Dogs that stray off the main paths may disturb birds and chicks, possibly killing them or breaking eggs. Species to look out for are Sky larks, Meadow pipits, Curlew, Red and Black grouse, Snipe and Pheasants.

Some if not all of these birds are declining in numbers, due partly to their vulnerability when nesting. Dogs are a threat to them, even if treading on them unintentionally. Some other threats are foxes, badgers, stoats, weasels, birds of prey and crows.

Please help to protect these birds during the nesting season by keeping your dog on the paths when walking in open areas such as grassland, moors, heathland and scrub.

Rivers

Some dogs love water and will think nothing of plunging into the river. With the extreme weather conditions over the last few years, a river that may be safe for your dog to swim in can change in a matter of hours to become a swollen torrent that could wash your dog away. Please be careful when near rivers if there have been heavy periods of rain or if they look swollen or fast flowing. It is best to put your dogs on the lead, until you have assessed the situation.

4

Livestock

If you find that you need to cross a field with cattle or horses and they seem interested in you or your dog it is recommended within the Countryside Code to let your dog off the lead. Never try to get between livestock and your dog. Your dog will get out of a situation a lot more easily with speed than you can. It is usually only cattle with young calves that are a threat, or young heifers or bullocks that tend to get a little inquisitive. They will usually stop when they get close to you or your dog.

Most horses will come over for a fuss but a small proportion do have a problem with dogs. They may see them as a threat and will act to defend the herd. Horses that are out with a rider are completely different as they are not defending the herd, and as long as you keep a safe distance there should not be a problem.

Sheep are not a danger to you, but your dog can be a danger to them. Where sheep are grazing it is vital that you have your dog on a lead or under very close control. You will know your dog, but if you are unsure it is better to play safe and keep your dog on a lead. It is important always to have your dog on a lead when around lambs. Lambs have a higher pitched bleat and can be the size of a cat, and your dog may act differently amongst them.

Ticks

If you have been walking in areas where sheep graze you should check your dog for ticks. They must be removed as soon as possible. It is best to use tick tweezers, which are specially designed to remove the head and leg parts of the tick. Ticks can carry diseases and the longer they remain latched on to your dog the more the chance of spreading infections.

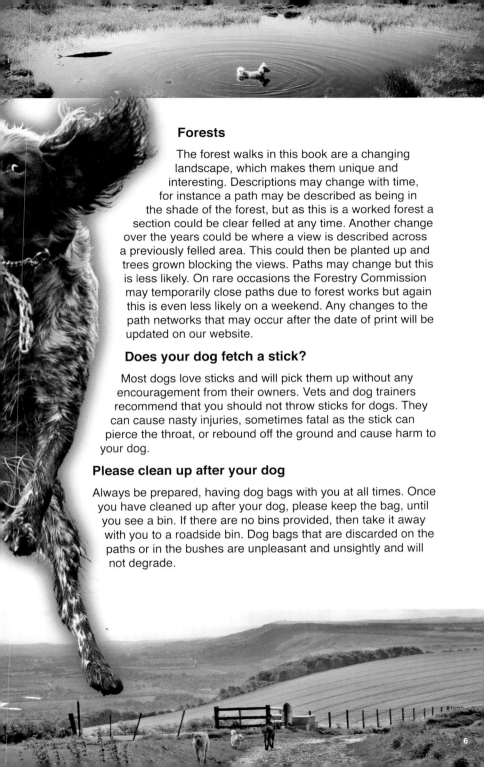

Forests

The forest walks in this book are a changing landscape, which makes them unique and interesting. Descriptions may change with time, for instance a path may be described as being in the shade of the forest, but as this is a worked forest a section could be clear felled at any time. Another change over the years could be where a view is described across a previously felled area. This could then be planted up and trees grown blocking the views. Paths may change but this is less likely. On rare occasions the Forestry Commission may temporarily close paths due to forest works but again this is even less likely on a weekend. Any changes to the path networks that may occur after the date of print will be updated on our website.

Does your dog fetch a stick?

Most dogs love sticks and will pick them up without any encouragement from their owners. Vets and dog trainers recommend that you should not throw sticks for dogs. They can cause nasty injuries, sometimes fatal as the stick can pierce the throat, or rebound off the ground and cause harm to your dog.

Please clean up after your dog

Always be prepared, having dog bags with you at all times. Once you have cleaned up after your dog, please keep the bag, until you see a bin. If there are no bins provided, then take it away with you to a roadside bin. Dog bags that are discarded on the paths or in the bushes are unpleasant and unsightly and will not degrade.

1. Chanctonbury Ring

Easy - 4 miles - 2hrs

This is a fairly short circular walk, but there is a steep hill to climb through beautiful woodland. After your climb you will join the South Downs Way, where you will have wonderful views across vast countryside. You will see the Iron Age hill fort named Chanctonbury Ring. Then after crossing the hilltop you descend into woodland again. There may be livestock grazing whilst out of the woodland. The descent can be slippery in wet weather on the chalk path. There is only a very short section of quiet country road.

How to get there - Take the Steyning (A283) turn-off, off the A27 Shoreham by-pass, just outside Brighton. Continue on this road, which by-passes Steyning. Look for the brown sign for Chanctonbury Ring, just after passing Wiston House. Follow the sign, turning left and continue along the minor road, where you will see the car park on your left.

Grid Reference – TQ 145124
Nearest Postcode – BN44 3DN

Parking – Free in the car park

Facilities – There are no facilities

You will need – Dog lead, dog bags, water for your dog

The Walk

❶ From the car park go back onto the road and turn left. Pass a lane on your right and on reaching the end of the tarmac road continue straight ahead onto a stony track. Pass beside a gateway and continue ascending gently. As you turn a sharp bend you will enter into mixed deciduous woodland.

The track gets quite rough in places with some gullies. Follow the path as it bends sharply to your left. Ignore a minor path on your left and continue ascending on the wide chalky path, which cuts across the hillside.

The woodland is beautiful, with lots of dead wood on the ground, which is fantastic for wildlife. As you reach close to the top of the hill you will leave the woodland behind. On reaching another path turn right, now on the South Downs Way. **❷** Walking with the woodland edge on your right and a stock fence on your left, with a field beyond.

The path begins to ascend once more, but only for a short distance. Keeping your dog under close control, pass through a small gate to avoid a cattle grid and then continue straight ahead, crossing the middle of a field. There may be sheep or cattle grazing.

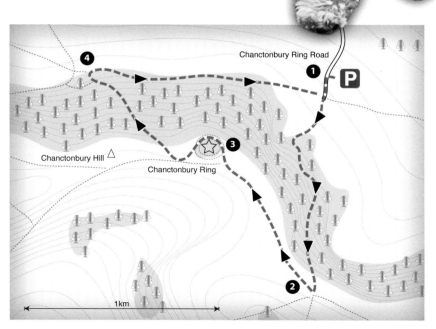

You will see the Iron Age hill fort named Chanctonbury Ring in the distance ahead, covered with trees. There are views on your left and right of the beautiful countryside.

❸ On reaching the ring take the path on your right, which follows the edge of the mound. You have stunning views on your right across endless countryside. Follow the path beside the edge of the trees. When you are almost half way around the ring you will see the open grassy area on your right. Head for the gate in the corner of a fenced field.

You will have sea views on your left. On reaching the gate pass through it and descend the grassy path beside the stock fence. There is a steep hillside on your right beyond the stock fence and trees and scrub on your left.

Pass through a gate and descend into woodland. The chalky path can be slippery if it is wet, and it is steep in places. If your dog has a good recall it would be better to let him off the lead to avoid him pulling you over. The wood becomes dense as you descend.

Ignore a path on your right. Shortly afterwards you follow beside a fence line on your right. Pass between two old gate posts and continue on the path descending through the woodland. On reaching a track turn right. ❹ You will reach three farm gates. Take the one at the end on your right. Continue beside the field on your left and the edge of woodland on your right.

The path veers away from the field as you enter back into woodland. The path snakes through the woodland and then follows the woodland edge once more. You will pass an old metal barn on your left, just after this pass through a gate ahead. Continue on the wide track with a field edge on your left. The track can be used by farm vehicles, so beware if your dog is running free.

On leaving the woods continue on a tree-lined path with fields on both sides, call your dog close, as there is a road ahead. You will reach a gate, pass through the gap beside the gate and continue to the road. Turn left and retrace your steps to the car park.

2. Cissbury Ring

Medium - 2.2 miles - 1hr 30min

This is a wonderful circular walk, which passes through meadows, woodland, scrub and farmland to reach an ancient hill fort. The walk continues around the perimeter bank of the hill fort, where you will have great views in all directions. There may be livestock grazing on parts of the walk.

How to get there – From Brighton take the A27 in the direction of Worthing and Portsmouth. Continue on the A27 until reaching the turn off for the A24 signed for London and Horsham. On reaching the outskirts of Worthing on the Findon Road (A24), look for the parking sign on your right for Cissbury Ring, turning onto May Tree Avenue. Take the first left-hand turn onto Storrington Rise, and just as you reach a right-hand bend in the road you will see the car park on your left.

Grid Reference – TQ 129077
Postcode – BN14 0HT

Parking – Free in Storrington Rise car park

Facilities – There are no facilities

You will need – Dog leads, dog bags, and water for your dog

The Walk

❶ Go to the furthest end of the car park, heading away from the road. Take the exit in the right hand corner of the car park. Follow the wider path on the left, crossing the meadow. Ignore a path on your right and continue on the wider grassy path.

On entering into the woods, take the path which veers to the left. Continue with the barbed fence on your left. Ascend the path, which bends to the left. Continue until reaching a kissing gate on your right. Put your dog on a lead or keep him under close control, as there may be sheep grazing. Pass through the kissing gate and turn left following the worn path through the wood pasture.

Continue straight ahead, passing the end of a fence line and gate on your left. You now leave the wood pasture and are in an open field, cutting across the hillside. You will see a fence line ahead, on reaching it continue straight ahead, with the fence on your left. The path ascends gradually.

Pass through a gate and continue straight ahead. Almost immediately you will meet another path, turn right here and follow the track. **❷** Go through the kissing gate on your right, just before the bend. Ascend on the path, which is steep with some steps. Take a breather on the way up so that you can look back and enjoy the views.

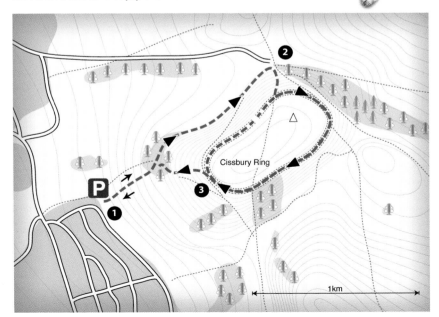

On reaching another path turn left to follow around the Cissbury Ring Iron Age Hillfort (watch out for rabbit holes as you go). There is scrub on your left and views of the sweeping hills ahead and to your left. Flowers on the banks add colour in the summer months, such as harebell and scabious.

On reaching a kissing gate on your left and another path on your right, take the path on the right ascending and then the path on the left, ascending the steps. You are now walking along the top path to the edge of the hill fort. The views are now extended and you can see the town of Worthing straight ahead and the sea beyond it.

Continue on this path, where you will see lots of colourful flowers in the meadows and on the banks during the spring and summer months. Cross another path and continue. You will pass the edge of woodland on your left with mature beech, ash and oak trees. Ascend over a mound and descend and then ascend the steps to continue along the well-worn path on the bank (rampart). You will pass some steps on your left and soon you will be walking in the opposite direction as you have almost turned full circle, and are now back on the other side of the fort.

The area on your right is hilly and scrubby. ❸ You will descend some steps on your left and then follow the worn path, where you will cross over a second mound to reach a kissing gate. Pass through the kissing gate and veer left, ignoring the two gates on your right.

Descend on the wider path furthest from the fence line on your right. Ignore a path on your left and continue to descend towards the trees. Ignore a gate on your right in the corner of the field and pass through the metal kissing gate straight ahead. Take the path on your right once you have reached an opening into meadows. Follow beside the woodland edge on your right. The path bends to the right into woods, then you will reach a familiar meadow. Continue straight ahead, descending across the meadow back to the car park.

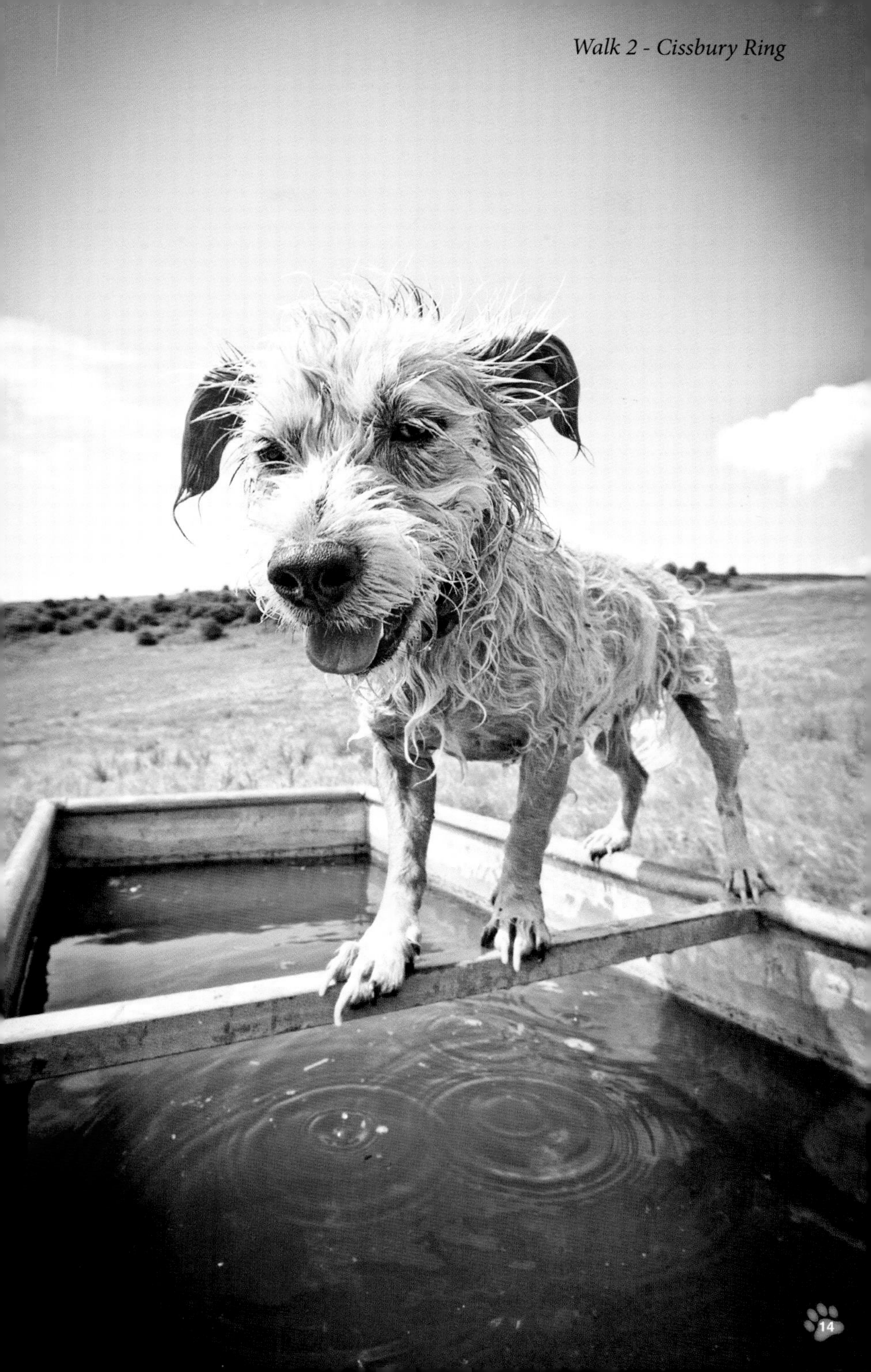

3. Church Hill

Medium - 3 miles - 2hrs

This is a stunning circular walk through beautiful woodland. You will pass along some quiet tracks, where you will have stunning views of the surrounding countryside. There is a quiet access road, which will lead to a livery yard and then a gradual ascent, passing alongside the edge of a forest. You will walk along bridleways, and therefore you may encounter horses.

How to get there – From Brighton take the A27 in the direction of Worthing. Continue on the A27 (Upper Brighton Road), passing through Worthing and following the sign for Arundel, Chichester and Portsmouth, continuing on the A27. On the outskirts of Worthing turn right, following a sign for High Salvington. Continue on this quiet road, turning left at the sharp bend onto Honeysuckle Lane. You will reach the car park at the end of the lane.

Grid Reference – TQ 119068
Nearest Postcode – BN13 3BT

Parking – Free in the Car Park

Facilities – There are no facilities

You will need – Dog leads, dog bags, and water for your dog

The Walk

1 From the car park go to the furthest end and follow the footpath, which passes the interpretation panel. You will have a large meadow on your left and scrub on your right. At the corner of the meadows you will pass another interpretation panel on your left and then leave the meadow area to enter into woodland.

Ignore a path on your left and continue straight ahead. On reaching another path turn left. You will have woodland on your left and a hedgerow on your right with farmland beyond it.

On reaching the end of the woodland you will have farmland on both sides, with a thick hedgerow on your right. Continue straight ahead passing an entrance into a field. You will now have a stock fence on your left. Another path will join the path that you are on, from your right.

Continue straight ahead, where you will now have trees on your right. There are livestock fields on your left. Ignore a path on your right. Pass an entrance into a field on your left. There is a barbed wire fence on your right. On reaching the end of the field on your left, you will enter into mixed deciduous woodland.

On leaving the woodland you will have views on your right of Cissbury Ring which is a Neolithic hill fort on the top of the hill. The views will open up as you

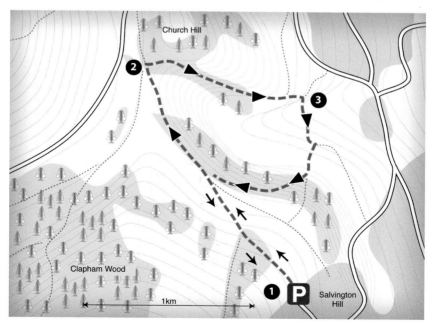

continue. ❷ Take the path on your right, just before you begin to descend, which is a bridleway.

The path ascends to begin with, passing a field entrance on your left and then entering into woods. The path then descends, gently to begin with, beside a stock fence on your right. There is a barbed wire fence on your left. You will reach a flint wall on your left and a tree lined field edge on your right.

The path will descend quite steeply in places. Call your dog close to your or put him on a lead, as the gradient lessens you will reach some houses on your left and there is an access road. Ignore the footpath on your left and continue past the houses.

Descend to the access road and turn right. ❸ Follow the concrete road, passing houses. Descend to the farm yard passing a parking area on your left. Turn left immediately afterwards and before reaching the house straight ahead. Turn right again almost immediately. Follow the path and just before reaching a horse paddock on your right, take the path on the right and ascend with the horse paddock on your left.

On reaching another path turn right into woodland. There is a barbed wire fence on your right and the path ascends gradually. A little further along the path reaches the woodland edge with fields on your left. Continue on the path, passing a farm gate on your right as you enter back into woodland.

On reaching another path turn left and continue on this path, ignoring a path on your left and then a little further along, ignore a couple of paths on your right. On reaching a tarmac road turn right into the car park.

4. Kithurst Hill

Easy - 2.4 miles - 1hr 30min

This is a beautiful walk, with wonderful scenery and quiet paths, and farmland on each side. You will be met with amazing views across a steep-sided field, which flattens suddenly where the views continue across endless farmland and woodland. You will then continue on the edge of the sloped field. On the return path you will walk part of the South Downs Way long-distance route.

How to get there – Take the A283 from Storrington, heading towards Petworth and Pulborough. Immediately after passing a sign for Southdown Gliding Club take the next left on Clay Lane. Turn right at the end of Clay Lane and take the next road on your left, which is a no-through road. You will reach the car park at the end of the road.

Grid reference – TQ 070124

Parking – Free in the car park

Facilities – There are no facilities

You will need – Dog lead, dog bags and water for your dog

The Walk

❶ From the car park, go back to the entrance, turn left and then immediately turn right, where you will pass a finger post on your left. Continue on the track, passing beside a vehicle barrier. Continue straight ahead and then leave the track, passing beside a gate on your left to join a path between fences, which is indicated by a blue way-marker.

You will have extensive views on your left. Continue between the fields. Trees line the path in places. You will begin to ascend. Continue on the path, where you will reach an opening at the end of the field on your left. There is a finger post on your right and two field gates on your left. Continue straight ahead, ignoring the paths on your left and right.

Continue to ascend between the fences and fields. As you ascend you will gain views on your right, across the fields to the hills in the distance. The area opens up where the fence on your left is set back away from the path. There are no trees here and the path is much wider. You will pass a trig point on your left and soon afterwards you will reach a gate. **❷** There may be livestock beyond the gate, so keep your dog under close control.

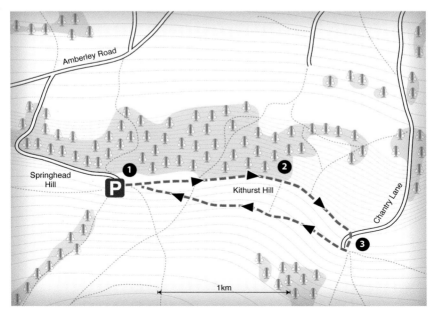

Pass through the gate and continue straight ahead on the edge of a sloping field, with some hillocks and scrub. Continue beside the stock fence on your right. The views are outstanding here, across the sloping field on your left to vast countryside below, with lots of woodland. There are views on your right of sloping fields and the sea beyond.

Descend the path, staying next to the fence line. You will pass some scrubby areas, which will impede your view for a short distance. Ignore a path marked by a finger post on your left, and continue to descend. A little further along you will pass a farm gate on your right.

You will reach a gate; pass through it, putting your dog on a lead. Continue to the road. Cross the road and ascend the bank opposite. Pass through another gate and continue on the worn path through the small field, keeping your dog under close control in case there are livestock.

❸ You will reach a kissing gate and a finger post. Pass through the kissing gate, keeping your dog under close control. Turn right and continue on the edge of a small car park.

You are now on the South Downs Way long-distance footpath. Pass a quiet road on your right and continue straight ahead, where you will pass between the post and rail fence with a timber box frame below. Continue between the fields, where wild flowers and grasses line both sides of the path in the summer months. A little further along the path widens out, with scrub and young trees on your left. Pass a bridleway on your right and you will then have stock fence on your left.

There are views on your left across the landscape. Pass another bridleway on your left and right and continue straight ahead, between the field boundaries, which are tree-lined. At the end of a field on your right you will pass a small gate. Continue a little further and take the next turning on your right, beside the metal gates, to reach the car park entrance.

5. Rackham Banks

Medium - 4 miles - 2hr 30min

This is a super walk, which includes part of the South Downs Way long-distance footpath. You will reach stunning views, as you walk between fenced farmland. The famous rolling hills can be seen, as many hills roll down to collide with one another in the valley below. There is a gradual hill to climb on the edge of farmland, where you will have views across the hills to the sea. On your return you will then walk on the edge of broadleaved woodland.

How to get there – Take the A283 from Storrington, heading towards Petworth and Pulborough. Immediately after passing a sign for Southdown Gliding Club, take the next left on Clay Lane. Turn right at the end of Clay Lane and take the next road on your left, which is a no-through road. You will reach the car park at the end of the road.

Grid Reference – TQ 070124
Nearest Postcode – RH20 1PR

Parking – Free in the car park

Facilities – There are no facilities

You will need – Dog lead, dog bags and water for your dog

The Walk

❶ Go to the furthest end of the car park and take the path on the left hand side. You will reach a well-made wider path where you should turn right. You are now on the South Downs Way long-distance path. Continue between the farm fields, with views on your left and right of the beautiful countryside and the sea in the distance on your left.

Head towards the woodland strip that stretches across the width of the field on your left. Just after passing between the trees you will reach a fork and a finger post. Take the path on the right, staying on the South Downs Way.

Ignore a kissing gate on your right soon after. Continue on the path, which is now grassy. There is hawthorn lining the path on your right, and the field on your right slopes away. As you continue the views open up ahead of you and are outstanding on a clear day.

You will pass a trig point on your left in the field. You will now descend and pass a finger post. Ignore the paths on your left and right and continue straight ahead. Descend a little further,

Turnpike Road

Rackham Hill

❷

❸

Springhead Hill

❶

P

1km

whilst enjoying the panoramic views before you.

Pass through a gate straight ahead and descend once again towards a large farmyard below. The path widens and becomes quite steep. At the bottom of the hill you will reach a finger post, just before the gate onto the farm track. ❷ Leave the South Downs Way here and turn left and back on yourself. Follow the sign for the restricted byway.

Pass through the small gate on your right and ascend on the wide chalk track. Ignore the bridleway, which veers to your right. Continue on the track. There is a grassy, scrubby bank on your left with spring and summer flowers and views across the countryside on your right.

You will soon be walking through a large field. You can see a triangular section of woodland ahead. Pass through the gateway into another field. Continue on the right hand side of the field edge with a wire fence on your right. The track is now grassy. There is a lovely sloping field and a woodland bank on your right. This is known as Rackham Banks.

On reaching the woodland go through the gate on your left (not the farm gate straight ahead). Turn right and ascend beside the woods on a narrow grassy path. On leaving the woods you will reach a finger post. Continue straight ahead, staying on the byway.

There is a field on your left and a thick overgrown hedge on your right. Summer flowers line the path on both sides. The path begins to descend gradually and there are views on your right where the trees allow.

On reaching another path and finger post turn left. Ascend gradually on the wide track to the edge of a field. There is a fence line on your right with a field on the other side. ❸ The track will bend to the right when you reach the woodland on a familiar path. Ignore the path on your left and continue on the South Downs Way. You will reach the car park further along on your left.

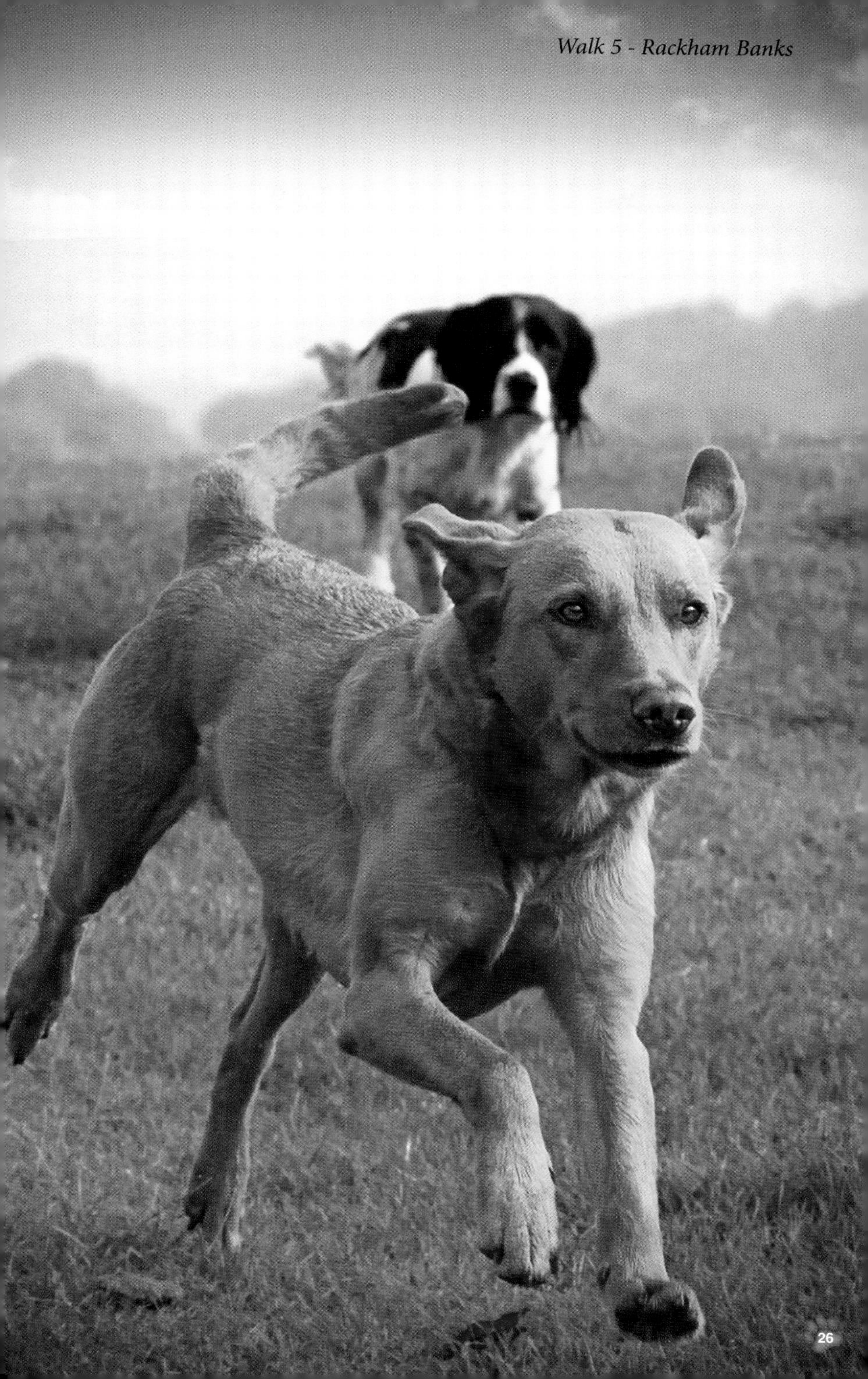

6. Pulborough Reserve

Easy - 1.6 miles - 1hr

This walk passes through mixed deciduous woodland and pine trees. There are open areas of gorse, scrub and heather, with sandy paths. You will pass some fenced areas within the reserve, which are there to protect the wildlife habitats. A slight ascent brings wonderful views across the reserve and beyond.

How to get there – From Pulborough Village take the A283 signed for Storrington. The reserve is located on the right-hand side soon after passing the turn off, for Racham on your left.

Grid Reference – TQ 058164

Postcode – RH20 2EL

Parking – Free in the reserve

Facilities – There is a visitor centre, toilets, a shop and a café

You will need – Dog lead, dog bags and water for your dog

The Walk

❶ From the car park, head towards the visitor centre. After passing the last car park, and before reaching the path to the visitor centre, turn left following the sign for Heathland. On reaching another path you will see a notice board. Turn left on this path, which has split rail fencing on your left, and continue through the mixed woodland.

Pass an entrance to the car park on your left and continue straight ahead. Ignore a second entrance to the car park and follow the path, which bends sharply to your right. On reaching another path (which isn't clear in the woodland, but there is a small sign to the visitor centre) turn right.

Descend through the woods, on a sunken, sandy path, ignoring minor paths on your left and right. Another path will merge with the path that you are on from your left. Don't allow your dogs to breach the fencing on your left, as this is a wildlife reserve.

The path will join another path on your right. Continue straight ahead, between the stock fences. As you continue the stock fence

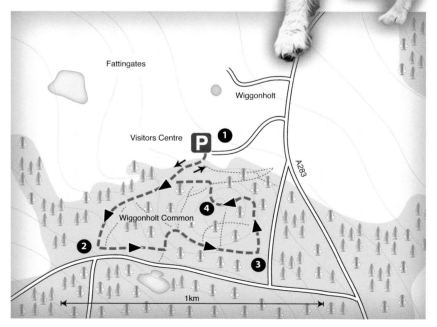

will veer away on your left. The path has a gentle ascent. On reaching the end of the fence on your right, turn left. **❷** There is a road on your right, which runs parallel to the path, and there are no boundary fences, so keep your dog under close control or on a lead. The road isn't busy, but the cars travel at speed.

Ignore a path on your left and then you will reach a stock fence on your left, which continues alongside the path. Continue past an entrance into the reserve. The path turns left, following the fence line. There is also another road which runs parallel to the path, so, again, keep your dog under very close control or on a lead.

❸ The fence turns another corner and the path veers to your left. Your dog is safe again to be let off the lead here, as you will leave the road behind. The path is wider here. After about 10 metres you will reach another path. Turn left and then ascend towards a gate, ignoring a path on your right. Continue to the gate, but don't go through it. Turn right into an open area and ascend gradually.

❹ You will pass a seating area, which over looks the reserve. Continue on this path, which bends to the right. Pass under mature beech and oak trees. You will pass another seating area on your left, which overlooks the reserve and to views beyond.

Continue on the path, which descends to reach another path. Turn left and continue to descend on a sunken path. When you reach another path turn right. Ascend now on a familiar path. Turn left on reaching another path, which isn't well-defined but there is a finger post a little further along.

Just before reaching an entrance into the car park turn left again and follow the signs back to the visitor centre.

7. Lord's Piece

Easy - 1 mile - 45min

This is a wonderful short circular walk, where you will pass through heathland and woodland, dominated by Scots pines and oak trees. There is also a pond where your dog can cool off in hot weather. The paths are mainly sandy underfoot. After a gentle ascent, you will be rewarded with beautiful views across the wooded hillside and beyond. In the summer months you will hear chirping from the many crickets living on the common.

How to get there – From Petersfield take the A272 signed for Midhurst. Continue on the A272 after passing Midhurst, now following the sign for Petworth. Continue into Petworth and turn left on the A285 following the sign for Chichester. Turn left when you see the sign for Bignor, Sutton, Coates and Burton Mill. Shortly after passing Burton Mill and the lake on your left you will continue straight ahead at the cross roads. A little further on, pass a road on your right, which is sign posted for West Burton. The car park will be just beyond the turn-off, on your right hand side.

Grid Reference – SU 989174

Parking - Free in the car park

Facilities – There are no facilities

You will need – Dog lead, dog bags

The Walk

1 From the car park, pass through the kissing gate beside the notice board. Take the first grassy path straight ahead, not the main path on the left. The path will descend and you will see the boundary fence on your right. The heath/grassland expands on your left.

You will pass a farm gate on your right. The path veers away from the road and the boundary fence. The path veers left a little before reaching the farm gate. You will see a pond; follow the path, which leads to the pond edge.

2 Continue past the pond, where you will reach another path. Turn right and on reaching a fork turn left, just before reaching another car park. The path becomes a faint grassy path. Ascend gradually on a white, sandy path. It is dominated with bracken here. On reaching a fork, turn left and continue to ascend up the bank, towards the Scots pine trees.

Turn left on reaching another path, almost at the top of the hill. You will have views now over the tops of trees for miles. There are mature oaks and Scots pines, which are well-spaced standard trees. The path is level here. Pass between raised banks. Ignore

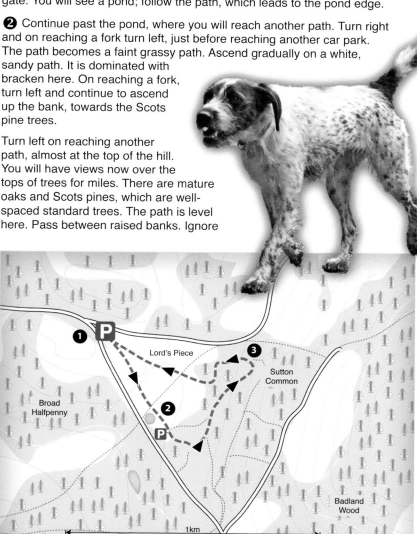

paths on your left and right and continue straight ahead, where you are now in an open area.

Just before you reach some trees, the path veers to your left. Take the sandy path on your left, just before reaching a fence ahead. There are stunning views ahead of the wooded hillside. Bracken dominates the heath again here. Ignore a narrow path on your left and veer right. ❸ You will reach a house and garden. Turn left and stay on the narrow sandy path.

Take the path on the left, just before reaching a fork. Descend on the white sandy path, passing between Scots pines. Continue on the path as it bends to your right. Ignore a path on your right, which ascends towards pine trees, and take the next path on your right just after.

Cross another path and continue straight ahead. Continue on this path, which will lead back to the car park.

8. Bignor Hill

Medium - 5 miles - 3hrs 30mins

This is a super circular walk, with spectacular views after only a little ascent. You will be walking alongside arable fields and between stone walls on a wide long-distance path, the South Downs Way. Your return will be through the delightful Houghton Forest in the shade of trees, both broadleaved and coniferous.

How to get there – From Arundel, take the A284 signed for Pulborough, London and Dorking. At the roundabout continue to follow Pulborough on the A29. When you see the sign for West Burton and Bignor, turn left. Continue to follow the signs for Bignor and Sutton (not Bignor Park). Pass the sign for the Roman Villa on your right. You will then reach Bignor Village. Pass a road on your right, and then take the left bend just after. Continue past the farm buildings and farmyard and ascend on the single track road, where you will reach the car park at the top of the hill on your left.

Grid Reference – SU 973129

Parking – Free in the National Trust car park

Facilities – There are no facilities

You will need – Dog lead, dog bags and water for your dog

The Walk

❶ From the car park face the road and turn right. Go to the end of the car park and take the wide path straight ahead, which veers away from the road. You are now on the South Downs Way (SDW) long-distance footpath. Ascend between open arable fields on a flint path, where you will soon have views on your right.

There is a belt of trees on your left across from the field. As you reach the top of the hill the views are terrific, stretching for miles in all directions. You then descend, passing a memorial stone on your left. **❷** There is now a stock fence on your left with grazing pasture beyond.

As you descend the panoramic views will continue. Stay on the wide path as it bends sharply to your left, ignoring the track straight ahead. The path descends quite steeply here with ash trees on each side of the path.

Follow the finger post directions, staying on the SDW as you turn a series of sharp bends. On returning to a straight path, pass a farm outbuilding on your left and continue. The path now begins another ascent.

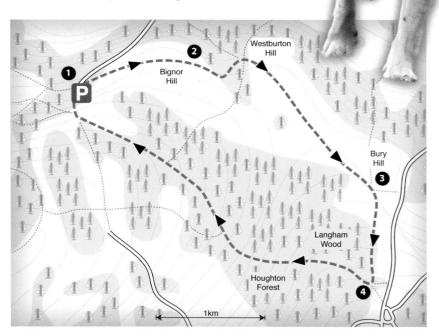

Continue between the fields with wild flowers and herbs lining the path on each side. As you continue you will eventually see woodland on your far right. The path will eventually reach the woodland edge.

On reaching the woodland edge you will see a finger post. Turn right on the narrow path, which is signed as a bridleway. ❸ You have now left the SDW. Continue with the woodland edge on your right and an open arable field on your left for quite a distance. You will hear a busy road ahead, but you will turn off before reaching it.

As you come under the shade of the trees the path bends sharply on your left. Before going around the bend take a narrow path on your right to enter into Houghton Forest. Descend on the path and, shortly after, you will reach a wider track. ❹ Turn right here, where you will follow the Denture Monarch's Way.

Take the next left, following the blue way-marker, and then almost immediately cross another path and continue straight ahead. Continue on this path for some distance, ascending through the mixed woodland, which is dominated by beech trees at this point.

Ignore any minor paths on your left and right and continue on the wide path. When the path levels out, you will enter a woodland clearing. The Forestry Commission are working with Butterfly Conservation to help protect the rare pearl-bordered fritillary butterfly, by creating woodland glades. The glades provide light to encourage wood violets, which the larvae require.

Continue through the glade and then ignore a bridleway on your left. The path becomes a little narrower here as the trees enclose it, giving welcome shade for your dog on a hot day. As you ascend once again the trees are dominated by ash with silver birch and hazel.

Ignore a path on your right and continue straight ahead. The woods are now dominated by hazel coppice. Ignore a path on your right and continue. Pass a path on your left and shortly after it, pass a forest track on your right. Continue on the path, where you are now on the edge of the woodland, with a field on your right.

You will pass a National Trust sign for Bignor Hill. Ignore a path on your left, and you will reach a stock fence on your right with a woodland clearing on your left, with some gorse at the edge. On reaching a finger post and another path, turn right. Continue with a field edge on your right and woodland on your left. Keep your dog under close control, as the car park is a little further along on your right.

9. Eartham Woods   Medium - 5.6 miles - 3hrs 30mins

This is a stunning walk, firstly through meadows and farmland, with lovely views across the beautiful countryside and passing amongst some wonderful parkland trees and scrub. You will then enter into the forest, where you will follow the wide tracks. There are some broadleaved trees amongst the conifers. There may be cattle and sheep for part of the walk.

How to get there – From Arundel, take the A284 signed for Pulborough, London and Dorking. At the roundabout continue to follow for Pulborough on the A29. Turn left on seeing the sign for West Burton and Bignor. Continue to follow the signs for Bignor and Sutton (not Bignor Park). Pass the sign for the Roman Villa on your right. You will then reach Bignor Village. Pass a road on your right, and then take the left bend just afterwards. Continue past the farm buildings and farmyard and ascend on the single-track road, where you will reach the car park at the top of the hill on your left.

Grid Reference – SU 973129

Parking – Free in the car park

Facilities – There are no facilities

You will need – Dog lead, dog bags, water for your dog

The Walk

❶ From the car park, face the road and turn left. Keeping your dog under close control, pass through a gate ahead and to your left, to enter into farmland. There may be cattle and sheep. Continue on the grassy path. You will briefly pass a stock fence on your left. Stay on the path straight ahead, ignoring a path which veers to your left.

Continue on the grassy path through the middle of a meadow. Cross another path and continue straight ahead. Pass through the trees, and on reaching another path, cross it to continue straight ahead. **❷** Pass through a gate, following the sign, on reaching a finger post for Gummer's Bothy.

You will have views on your left and trees on your right. On reaching another finger post, continue straight ahead on the public footpath. You will follow a raised bank on your right. As you continue you will gain lovely views straight ahead.

Descend to a finger post and ignore the footpath on your left. Continue straight ahead, following the sign for the bridleway.   Walk along the ridge, at the edge of the field. As you continue, the path will be beside the ridge on your left. You will see a farm building on your left and descend on the path.

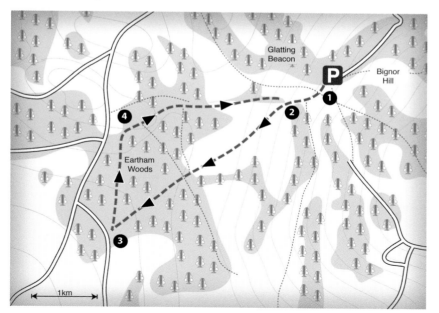

Pass the entrance to Gumber's Bothy and farm and continue straight ahead. Pass though the gate and ascend on the path beside the ridge. The views expand as you continue. Descend again to a gate and pass through it. Continue straight ahead on the worn path between the trees, with a stock fence on your left below the bank. The trees are remnants of an old hedge, with hawthorn, elder and ash standards. As you continue there is a belt of hazel coppice.

You will pass through another gate, into woodland. On reaching another path and finger post, continue straight ahead descending on the track, the Monarch's Way, through the beech-dominated woodland. The path is undulating and you continue straight ahead, crossing another track. The track is wide, allowing sun to reach the ground in places.

As you continue, you will cross another track. The trees meet above you here and there is a road ahead, so keep your dog under close control. On reaching a finger post and another path, turn right, now walking in the opposite direction to the road and leaving the Monarch's Way. ❸ Continue on the well-made gravel path. Ignore a path on your left, soon after. You will pass a couple of copper beech trees, which are dark purple in colour.

Ignore the paths on your left and right and continue straight ahead. As the path bends sharply to your right, continue straight ahead. Follow the narrow path through the woods, which ascends. Continue straight ahead, passing a left and right turn. There is now hazel coppice on your left and beech trees on your right. As you continue to ascend, the hazel gives way to the beech.

The path merges with another from your right. Continue straight ahead, leaving the path which bends to your right. You will pass the end of a post and rail fence to reach another track. Turn right here and continue on the path on the edge of woodland. There is a field on your left and the path will ascend gently.

Ignore a path on your right and continue straight ahead, leaving the field edge. You will now be back in the woodland. The path bends slightly and you will pass another path on your right. Continue straight ahead on the sunken path, between banks. Pass through an old disused vehicle barrier. The path is firmer here and will eventually level out.

Ignore a forest track on your right and just afterwards ignore a path on your left. Pass a gate on your right and continue on the path straight ahead. ❹ On leaving the woodland, continue on the path, now between open arable fields. There are two aerial masts in the distance on your left.

On reaching a finger post on your left and a small wood continue straight ahead. You will have views on your right. Continue on this level path for quite a distance. As the path bends sharply to your left continue straight ahead, following the sign on the finger post for Gumber's Bothy.

There is now a small wood on your right and a field edge on your left. Soon afterwards ignore a farm track on your right. Continue beside a stock fence on your left, with mixed broadleaved woodland on your right. Pass through a gate ahead and continue straight ahead, where you are now at a familiar spot. Continue straight ahead, ignoring the paths on your left and right.

Pass through the gate ahead and continue in the woodlands. Ignore a track on your right and continue straight ahead. There is a field on your right and woodland on your left. Turn left shortly afterwards to follow the sign for the bridleway. Pass through a gate and continue straight ahead on the grassy path between the trees.

On passing another finger post, continue straight ahead. Continue straight ahead on reaching a way-marker, where the path will merge with another. You will soon reach a familiar gate and the car park beyond it.

10. Lavington Common
Easy - 1.3 miles - 1hr

This circular walk is a mix of woodland and heathland. There are many rhododendrons, which look stunning in early summer when they are in flower; similarly the heather is wonderful during July and August when it flowers. There is a pond near the end of the walk, where your dog can cool off. There are no roads and no livestock; however, during nesting season, there may be ground nesting birds, so it is better to keep your dog on the path.

How to get there – From Petersfield take the A272 signed for Midhurst. Continue on the A272 after passing Midhurst, now following the sign for Petworth. Turn right on seeing the sign for Graffham. Continue on this road, ignoring the turn off for Graffham on your right. The car park will be on your left hand side shortly after.

Grid Reference – SU 949187

Parking – Free in the National Trust car park

Facilities – There are no facilities

You will need – Dog leads, dog bags

The Walk

1 Make your way to the notice board in the car park. Take the path straight ahead, and pass through pine trees. You will soon be in the open heathland on a sandy path. There are silver birch and Scots pine trees regenerating and some mature standards.

Stay on the path through the middle of the heath and head towards the pine forest. Pass beside a stile to enter the forest. Rhododendrons dominate the ground canopy. Turn left on the wide path and continue, taking the next path on your right. **2**

There is a lot of bracken dominating the ground here, with some holly and rhododendron. Pass a path on your right, and then after this silver birch trees dominate on your right and Scots pine on your left.

When you see paths on your left and right, take the right turn. The path begins to descend through mixed broadleaved woodland. Pass a path on your left and continue. **3** You will reach a wider path; turn right onto this path, to join the Serpent Trail. Ascend for a short distance and then descend.

You will pass through thick rhododendron and then holly, with silver birch dominating this section of the woods. Continue on a little further, where rhododendron and Scots pine dominate once more. You will reach a split rail barrier. Continue, passing through the barrier, where the path becomes quite narrow.

The path is slightly raised and you will cross over many tree roots. The trees thin out, and you will be walking on the edge of the heathland on your right. Ignore a path on your left and continue straight ahead, where you will enter back into woodland. You will pass a small pond on your right, and then continue straight ahead.

Take the next path on your right to enter back into the car park.

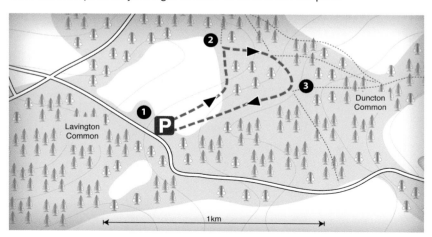

11. Petworth Park
Medium - 3 miles - 1hr 30mins

This walk is in the 700-acre grounds of the seventeenth-century house, which were designed by 'Capability' Brown. There are herds of fallow deer, which roam throughout the grounds. There are also many parkland trees, which look glorious as they have matured, with the space to stretch out their branches. You will pass two large ponds, of which the top pond has an old boathouse. The grounds are well cared for, with long grasses and meadows in places and some scrub. You will need to keep your dog under close control, as the deer may be anywhere and there may be ground nesting birds during March to July. There are no roads.

How to get there – From Petersfield take the A272, signed for Midhurst. Go through Midhurst and continue to Petworth. On reaching Petworth, take the A283 signed for Guildford and Northchapel. The car park for Petworth Park will be found on your left hand side further along the road.

Grid Reference – SU 966238   **Nearest Post Code** – GU28 9LR

Parking – Pay and display National Trust

Facilities – There are no facilities in the car park

You will need – Dog lead, dog bags

The Walk

❶ From the car park with your back to the entrance, make your way to the left hand corner furthest from the road. There are deer in the park, so keep your dog under close control or on a lead. There is more than one herd, so if you pass a group of deer there may be more elsewhere. Pass an interpretation panel on your right. Continue on the wider path amongst lovely open grassland, with mature parkland trees.

After about 150 yards, just after passing a hawthorn tree on your left, take the path which veers to your left. On meeting another path turn right. Continue on the path, with mature trees on your left, following the boundary wall roughly 100 yards away on your left. Ignore a path, which veers to your right. As you continue there are trees on both sides. There are some fabulous mature oaks amongst the trees.

You will reach the Lower Pond. Dogs can cool off here on hot days. **❷** On reaching the pond continue on the gravel path. Continue straight ahead, leaving the pond and staying within sight of the boundary wall. The wall kinks in and has metal railings on the top. After passing a house on your left, take a path which veers to your right and ascends a hill.

On reaching another path, turn right and then take the grassy path almost immediately on your right. Continue on the cut grassy path, which ascends as it crosses hilly pasture. On reaching the top you will gain views across the estate grounds and beyond in all directions.

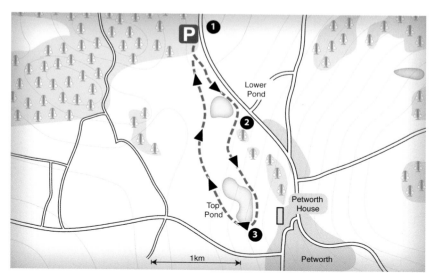

On reaching a path you will see two distinct paths on your left; take the second one. You will see the Top Pond on your right. Ascend a little further, passing many trees which will offer shade on hot days. Ignore a path on your right and continue. Ignore another path on your left. On reaching a left and right turn, turn right.

As you reach the trees on your left, take a narrow path on your right and descend towards the pond. On reaching another path turn left. Continue on the path, where you will see the grand house on your far left. You will continue beside the water's edge. Pass a statue in the water of a dog, looking out across the pond. Your dog can cool off in the water.

Pass a stone bench and continue to follow the edge of the pond. You can join a stone path as you continue. There are several benches along the way. As the path splits in two ahead, veer off the main path and continue on a grassy path staying close to the pond. ❸ The path continues about 100 yards from the pond, through the middle of grassland.

There is a boathouse on the opposite side of the pond. On reaching another path where you are close to the pond edge, turn right. There is a small pond on your left here beyond the trees. You will pass estate fencing at the end of the pond. Ignore a path left and continue. Where the estate fence bends sharply to your right, take a path on your left. Descend with grass banks on your far left and right. There are wonderful parkland trees ahead.

Ignore a minor path on your left as you near the trees and continue on the wider path. As the path bends to your right you will see Lower Pond. Pass a left and right turn and continue to a crossroads of wider paths, with the pond straight ahead. Take the second left path here, with the pond to your right. Continue on this wide path, ignoring the minor path ahead and to your right. Continue on this path, which will eventually reach the car park.

12. Black Down

Easy - 2 miles - 1hr 30mins

This is a spectacular circular walk. It is the highest point in the National Park, and there are fabulous views in many places, which stretch for miles across beautiful wooded landscape and farmland. There are heathland slopes, which look wonderful when the heather is in flower. Pine and silver birch are scattered throughout the area and you will pass through beech woodland. Cattle are used as a management tool, but they are used to dog walkers, and show little interest. There is water along the way for your dog. There are no roads.

How to get there – From Godalming take the A286, signposted for Haslemere. On reaching Haslemere follow the sign for Petworth (A283) on the B2131. Just as you leave the built up area turn right on Hastle Hill. On reaching the give way, continue straight ahead but veering to your left, onto Tennyson's Lane. Continue on this lane and ignore the first car park on your right. You will reach a sharp left bend. Turn right here, where you will see the Black Down National Trust sign and car park.

Grid Reference – SU 922306   **Nearest Post Code** – GU27 3BJ

Parking – Free in National Trust car park

Facilities – There are no facilities

You will need – Dog leads, dog bags

The Walk

1 Continue to the furthest end of the car park from the road. Ascend the hill and pass through a gate. There may be cattle of a quiet gentle breed, so keep your dog under close control. You are now amidst some wonderful broadleaved woodland, with mosses growing on the tree trunks. There is a viewing area with a bench, where you will see for miles. Face the view and turn right to join another path.

Soon you will pass another viewing area with a bench. Continue straight ahead on the worn narrow path through the mixed broadleaved and pine woodland. The paths have many exposed roots and you will cut across the wooded hillside.

There is bilberry and bramble growing prolifically on the woodland floor, and patches of heather. The path is undulating, and you will reach another bench with a view. Take the lower path on reaching the bench. Ignore a minor path on your right and continue straight ahead.

The path widens and is now sunken, with a ridge on your left. Beech trees dominate the woods here. The path narrows again for a short section through mixed woodland. It soon widens again and is once more surrounded by beech trees. Ascend on the path, with some steps, and turn left onto a main path. You are now on the Serpent Trail, which is a long-distance footpath.

You will soon reach a finger post. Ignore the path on your left and continue straight ahead through the mixed woodland. Continue on the edge of a small

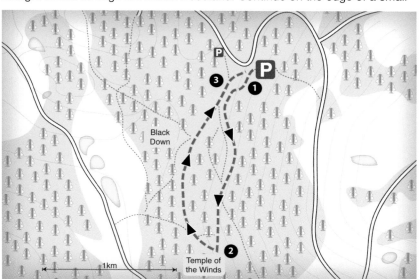

pond and ignore a path on your right just after. Ignore a minor path on your left and take the next path on your left and ahead, which is signed 'Temple of the Winds'. Keep to the left, where you will descend to a wonderful memorial seating area, and glorious views. ❷ There is a toposcope to direct your views. The views show off this woodland rich landscape.

Turn back the way you came and on reaching a fork veer to your left. On reaching another path and finger post, continue straight ahead. Ignore a path on your left immediately after. Continue on the main path in an open area with widely-spaced trees. Pass a bench on your right, where you will have stunning views across to Hampshire.

Ignore a path on your left and continue straight ahead. Ignore a second path on your left immediately after. There are some small water holes at the side of the path as you continue where your dog can cool off. There is a sloping hillside on your left with some heather. Heather dominates on your right with some pine and silver birch regenerating, and gorse patches. The views continue on your left. Ignore a path on your left, which cuts back in the opposite direction, and continue straight ahead. Ignore a path on your right and pass a bench just after it.

You will pass a bench on your left, with a toposcope to direct your views. Continue on the path. There is bilberry on your left and bracken on your right. Pine dominates here, with mixed, widely-spaced broadleaved trees. There are some small wet areas along the path, where your dog can cool off. On reaching a finger post, continue straight ahead. You will return to the woods. Ignore a path on your left and right and continue straight ahead.

A little further along there is a wet area on your left at the woodland edge, where your dog can have a cool off. At this point you will pass a finger post on your left, continue straight ahead here. Ignore a path on your left and then another path will merge with the path that you are on from your right.

Continue straight ahead, now descending on a sunken path back into mixed woodland. Soon afterwards take a path on your right indicated by a National Trust disc. Ascend over the mound, where you will reach a bench almost immediately, with stunning views of the beautiful landscape below. Face the view and turn left, passing the bench on your right. ❸

Continue on the narrow path, between bracken, on the edge of the hillside. You will soon descend on the path through woodland. On reaching another path turn left and soon you will pass through the gate to return to the car park.

13. Marley Common

Easy - 1 mile - 45mins

This is mostly a woodland walk, but you will pass through some grassland/ heath areas, where in the summer months there are many butterflies enjoying the summer flowers. There are a couple of wooded hills to climb, but nothing too steep. In the heathland areas there are cattle grazing, but they are a quiet breed and are used to dogs and their owners. There may be deer in the area. There are no roads.

How to get there – From the A3 between Godalming and Petersfield take the turn off for Haslemere and Midhurst on the A287. After passing through Haslemere, you will reach Kingsley Green. Continue through the village and on reaching the second cross roads, take the road on your right (which is unmarked, but the road on the left is Hatch Lane). Continue on this road, which narrows. You will pass a small car park on your left and a little further along, the car park will be on your right.

Grid Reference – SU 886311
Postcode – GU27 3PU

Parking – Donation box in car park

Facilities – There are no facilities

You will need – Dog lead, dog bags

The Walk

❶ From the car park go to the furthest end from the road, pass an interpretation panel on your right and go through a gate straight ahead. Continue on the path, which is a long-distance path called the Serpent Trail. Pass through a grassland clearing in the woods. On reaching a finger post continue straight ahead.

The path descends and you will reach and pass through a gate. Continue on the path through the woodland. Ignore a path on your left indicated by a way-marker, and continue. Ignore a path on your right, which isn't marked by a way-marker, and then ignore a path on your left next to a finger post. You will reach a way marker indicating straight ahead, but turn left here, where you leave the Serpent Trail behind. **❷**

Silver birch and holly dominate here. Ignore a path on your left and continue straight ahead. After you pass through the dense holly the path descends quite steeply. Pass through a gap in a bank and turn left to continue a steep descent. Ignore a path on your right and continue to the bottom. Ignore paths on your left and right and continue straight ahead to begin an ascent. The gradient is steep to begin with, but soon lessens.

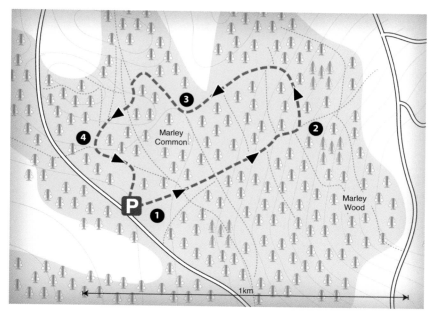

Continue on the path as it bends sharply to your right, **❸** through the mixed woodland. Ignore a path on your left, which is indicated by a red-topped post and continue straight ahead. The path narrows, and on reaching another wider path turn left. There is a bank on your right. On reaching another path, pass through the gate on your right and continue to follow the path.

Ignore a path on your right and take the wider path on your right just after, as you pass a way-marker on your left. Ignore a path on your right at a way-marker and continue straight ahead. Ignore a path on your left and continue straight ahead. There is an open area on your left. Ignore a path on your right and continue, past a way-marker. Pass a path on your left. Just before reaching a gate ahead, take a path on your left. **❹** You now re-join the Serpent Trail.

A path joins the path that you are on from your left. Continue on the same path that you are on through the clearing and ascend on the path. Another path will join from your left. At the fork take the path on your right, where you leave the Serpent Trail once again. Pass a bench on your left and then pass a wet boggy area on your right. Go through a gate, where you will return to the car park.

14. Woolbeding Common   Med 2.2 mile 2hrs

This walk starts with breath-taking views across a wooded slope to hills in the distance. As you walk along the edge of the hillside the views continue. You will pass under the shade of birch trees in places and between gorse scrub, where the views will come and go as you walk on sandy paths with some sandstone bedrock. There is heathland and woodland along the way, with a descent followed by a gradual ascent through the woods. There is the option of extending the walk across more open heathland, with scrub.

How to get there - From Petersfield, take the A272 heading towards Midhurst. Continue on this road until you see the sign for Woolbeding. Turn left here and continue on this lane until you see a sign for Older Hill. Turn right and continue on this road, where you will reach the car park on your right.

Grid Reference – SU 869259
Nearest Postcode – GU29 0QE

Parking – Free in the National Trust car park

Facilities – There are no facilities

You will need – Dog lead, dog bags and water for your dog

The Walk

❶ From the car park go back out onto the quiet road and cross to the opposite side. Continue to reach a bench where you will have lovely views. Take the path on your right, just before you reach the bench. There is bracken and some trees on both sides of the path.

You will soon descend on the path, where the views on your left can still be seen. The path becomes undulating. On reaching another path, turn left. This path is level to begin with. The views here on your left are spectacular. There is heather and bilberry on your right, with oak, silver birch and sweet chestnut woodland.

Ignore a path on your right, where you will see a trig point. You will begin to descend again here. Ignore a path on your left and keep to the right. You will reach a bench soon afterwards, where you will gain more views, also across the wooded landscape. **❷** Continue to descend on the path through the oak-dominated woodland.

Follow the obvious worn path, which descends, a little steeply in places. Ignore a path on your right and continue straight ahead. You will pass a house on your left, where you will reach a finger post. Turn right here and continue through the woodland. After a short distance, the path will ascend gently. You

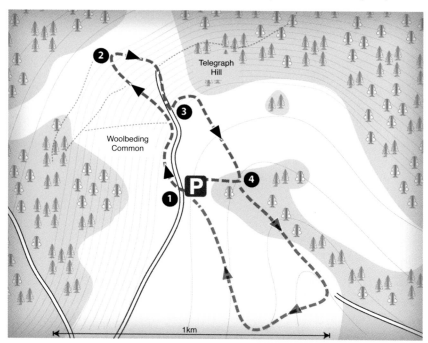

will reach a boundary fence on your left. Continue on the path, along the fence line.

You will reach a finger post on your right and a fork in the path. Take the path on your right. Continue between the banks, and the path will become quite steep. On reaching another way-marker, ignore the path on your right and continue straight ahead. Soon afterwards the path will descend. Put your dog on a lead or under close control, as you will reach an access road.

Pass a finger post on your right and continue straight ahead. You will pass a drive way here on your left. Continue between the banks through the woodland. On leaving the woods you will pass two driveways on your left. Continue straight ahead on the access track, which has a right-hand bend.

The track ascends and soon afterwards you will pass another finger post on your left; continue straight ahead. Ascend the quiet road, keeping your dog under close control or on a lead, and listen for cars. You are still between banks with woodland on both sides. Look out for a footpath on your left, marked with a finger post. You won't see the finger post until you turn off the road. ❸

Ascend to begin with and veer to your left. After passing the thick bracken you will ascend a little more steeply through the woods. On reaching a finger post, ignore the path on your left and continue straight ahead. You will soon reach an access track; turn right onto the track, keeping your dog under close control or on a lead. Almost immediately afterwards you will pass a finger post on your left. Continue straight ahead, descending gently. There is a hedge on your left, with an equestrian centre beyond it. ❹ On reaching another finger post on your left you have the option to extend your walk through an open heath area or to go back to the car park.

A. The Extended Walk.

Continue straight ahead, ignoring the track on your right. You will pass a path on your left, as you continue straight ahead. You will pass a track on your left, which gives access to Scotland Farm. Pass a path on your right and on reaching another finger post turn right.

Continue straight ahead, where shortly you will reach another finger post. Continue again straight ahead, through the silver birch woods. Cross another path and still continue straight ahead, amongst bracken. There is gorse and silver birch on your left and heather, silver birch and gorse on your right.

You will pass a finger post, where you should continue straight ahead and begin descending gently. Ignore paths on your left and right and continue straight ahead, where you will soon reach a wide path. Turn right here and pass a finger post and a path on your left, continuing on the wide path beneath the power lines.

There are trees on your left and an open area on your right, which is dominated by bracken. You will ascend gently, and as you continue you will pass the trees on your left and now have open areas on both sides. There are some gorse and heather amongst the bracken, with views on your left.

You will soon descend, and on reaching a fork take the path on your right. Descend to a track, which you cross, and take the path opposite to return to the car park.

B. Route straight to car park.

Turn right here and continue through the woods. The path soon descends between gorse. Take a path on your right, indicated by a finger post, and continue to descend between the bracken, through the woods. You will soon return to the car park.

15. Iping Common

Easy - 1.4 miles - 1hr 30min

This is a beautiful circular walk through lowland heath, which is wonderful in July and August when the heather is in flower. At times you will pass through the shade of silver birch and pine trees. There are some gradual ascents on sandy paths. You will have stunning panoramic views at the highest point of the walk. There is a pond, where your dog can cool down in hot weather. There are no roads, but there may be livestock at certain times of the year.

How to get there –From Petersfield, take the A272 sign posted for Midhurst. Pass through the villages of Rogate and Trotten. A little further along, turn right at the crossroads, following the sign for Elsted. You will reach the car park on your right hand side shortly after turning onto Elsted Road.

Grid Reference – SU 852219
Nearest Postcode – GU29 0PB

Parking – Pay and Display in the National Trust Mam Nick Car Park

Facilities – Free in the car park

You will need – Dog leads, dog bags

The Walk

1 From the car park go to the furthest end from the road and, with your back to the road, continue to the left hand corner. Take the path beside the notice board and interpretation panel. Ignore a path on your right just afterwards. Continue straight ahead through the silver birch trees, where bracken and bramble cover the ground.

Take a path on your left, which is marked for the Serpent Trail, a long-distance path. There is gorse on your right to begin with. The trees become widely spaced and there are views straight ahead as you cross the heath on the sandy path. The path descends and you continue straight ahead to return amongst the trees, which are pine and silver birch. You will pass a narrow path soon afterwards on your left. Your dog will find water from a pond about 20 yards up this path.

As you continue, bracken dominates. On reaching another path turn left. This is a wider path, with silver birch trees on both sides; the bracken thins out a little and is replaced with grasses. On reaching another path, which is wider again, turn left. As the sandy path becomes grassy you will reach a fork. Take the path on your left.

Continue through the open heath, with some trees and young regenerating silver birch and pines. After crossing the open heath you will return to a

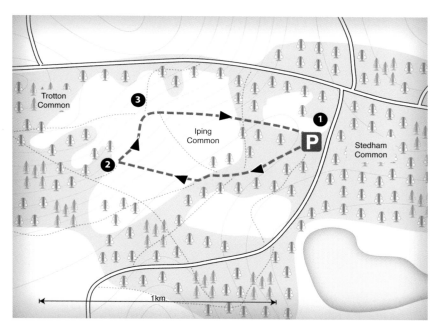

small woodland. Continue through the woods, where you will reach a bend to your right. You will see a concrete post at this point. Continue around the bend, to join a grassy track, ignoring the track straight ahead.

A little further along you will reach another sandy path. Turn left on this path, where you will have open heath again on your right and pines and silver birch regeneration on your left. There is pine woodland a little further ahead. On reaching a bend ignore a path on your left. Ascend on the sandy path. The path bends to your right to meet with another wide sandy path.

Continue to ascend with the pine woods on your left and heathland on your right. On reaching the top of the hill, ignore the path on your right. Look behind you here, where you can admire the wonderful views. ❷ Soon afterwards take a path on your right, which is marked by a way-marker with several blue arrows.

You now leave the Serpent Trail. The path is level, with bracken and gorse on both sides. After passing the gorse on your left you will have views ahead and to your left. Ignore the path on your right just after. There is open heath on your left and gorse and bracken on your right. The gorse and bracken clear on your right, where you will see the open heath now on both sides, with views in all directions.

You will reach another path. ❸ Turn right on this path and descend gently to begin with. There are widely-spaced trees on your right and trees beyond the heather on your left. Continue on this path for some distance. You will reach a bend/turn on your right. Ignore this and continue straight ahead on the grassy path. The path narrows a little between the gorse with silver birch trees.

As you continue there is open heath beyond the trees on your left. Further along, the trees close in. The path will bend to your right, where you will then reach the car park.

16. Westdean Woods   Med- 3.3 miles - 2hrs 30min

This walk begins on part of the South Downs Way long-distance trail and ascends gradually for some distance between farmland. You will be rewarded with wonderful views of the beautiful landscape. The walk continues through a lovely quiet forest with some mixed broadleaved trees. There are no roads or livestock, but there are deer in the area.

How to get there – Take the A286 from Midhurst heading in the direction of Chichester. After passing through the village of Cocking look out for Cocking Hill car park on your right.

Grid Reference – SU 875166

Parking – Free in the Cocking Hill car park

Facilities – There is a café and tea room opposite the car park

You will need – Dog leads, dog bags and water for your dog

The Walk

❶ Keep your dog on a lead to begin this walk, as the road from the car park is busy. From the car park, go to the furthest end from the entrance and leave the car park. Turn left on the access road, between hedgerows. This track is part of a long-distance route, the South Downs Way (SDW). There is grazing land on both sides, and views of the downs and woodlands ahead.

Stay on this path, passing a flint stone barn on your left and agricultural barns. There is a small paddock and a house on your right. You will then pass between hedgerows once again. Ascend on the track, keeping your dog under close control, as there may be farm vehicles and open entrances into fields ahead.

Pass Warren Bottom on your left and continue straight ahead. The hedgerow is replaced with grass banks and standard trees. Continue to ascend. On reaching a finger post, continue straight ahead, passing a large boulder. Have a look behind you, where you will be rewarded with stunning views.

There is an open field now on your left and a stock fence on your right with a field beyond it. The gradient lessens now as you come close to the summit.

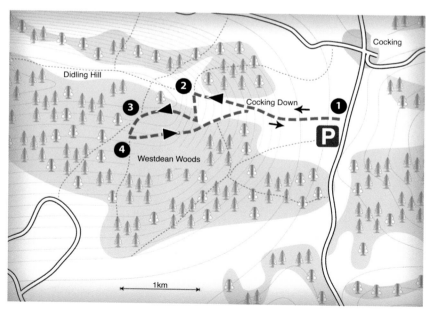

The next field on your right has a barbed fence. On reaching a second finger post, turn left. ❷ You now leave the SDW. Continue on a bridleway heading toward the trees.

Continue on a grassy track between fields. You will reach a wood on your right. On reaching a finger post turn right, entering into the forest. Ignore paths left and right just afterwards and continue straight ahead on the grassy track. Pass a large boulder on your right, where you cross a track. Descend on the path, which becomes steep. The path is now undulating. On reaching another finger post, continue straight ahead.

Ignore a track on your left and continue straight ahead. ❸ You will reach a track with a finger post on your left. Turn left on the track and left again immediately after, following the bridleway. The path descends slightly through the forest. ❹ On reaching another boulder, turn left. Ignore a track on your left and continue straight ahead, descending on the grassy track between new plantations.

Pass a finger post and ascend steeply. Ignore a path on your right and pass a finger post. Ignore a path on your left and continue straight ahead. Cross a track and continue straight ahead. On reaching another finger post and a track, turn left. Continue to ascend, and on reaching a boulder and another track turn right. Continue beside the field edge, with the forest on your right. Ignore a path on your right on reaching another finger post, and continue straight ahead.

On leaving the field edge, descend gradually into mixed woodland on your left and conifers on your right. Pass a vehicle barrier and continue straight ahead. As you leave the trees on your right there are views across the Downs. Soon you will have fields on both sides and views ahead. There are wild flowers in the summer months on both sides of the path.

You will reach another boulder and a familiar farm track. Turn right here, where you retrace your steps, descending between the fields. Keep your dog under close control as the busy road is ahead.

17. St Roche's Hill

Easy - 1.1 miles - 1hr

This is a short circular walk and as soon as you arrive at the car park there are wonderful views across beautiful sloping hills to the sea and the Isle of Wight. With very little effort you will have amazing panoramic views as you reach the Iron Age Hill fort, known as The Trundle. You will pass through a small woodland and then across the down. There are views throughout the walk. There are no roads, but there may be livestock.

How to get there - From Chichester, take the A286 signed for Lavant and Midhurst. Pass through Lavant and continue on the A286. After passing through West Dean Village and on the outskirts of Singleton Village turn right, following the sign for Goodwood and Open Air Museum. At the bend in the road, turn right just after the house with iron gates onto the unmarked lane. You will find the car park at the end of the lane.

Grid Reference – SU 871110
Nearest Postcode – P018 0PT

Parking – Free in Goodwood car park

Facilities – There are no facilities

You will need – Dog lead, dog bags and water for your dog in hot weather

The Walk

1 You will immediately be met with fantastic views across this dramatic scenery. From the car park face the views and turn left on a path which follows the edge of the car park. On reaching the gate, ignore a path on your right, but continue to follow the way-marker signed for New Lipchis Way, which ascends toward a mast.

There are stunning views on your right, between stock fences with fields on both sides. You will see the mound ahead, which is the perimeter of the ancient hill fort. You can choose to walk around the perimeter of the fort and head back the way you came or for a slightly extended walk, continue straight ahead, crossing through the middle. **2** As you ascend you will have amazing views on your left, of the hilly patchwork of fields and woodlands.

Ignore a path on your right and continue straight ahead. As you descend, the views open up straight ahead. You will see to Goodwood racecourse and beyond. Pass between the banks of the hill fort and turn right. Head towards the woods with the racecourse on your far left. Continue around the bottom of the mound and look for a way-marker on your far left to the edge of the woods. Cross the grassland to reach the way-marker and gate. **3**

Pass through the gate and enter the woods. Continue on the worn path close to the woodland edge, beside the fence line. The path becomes quite steep as you leave the fence. On meeting another path turn right, and ascend through the mixed woods, which are ash-dominated. Ignore a path on your right and continue, where you will reach a gate. Pass through the gate, keeping your dog under close control or on a lead, and veer left a little but straight ahead. There may be livestock grazing, but also ground-nesting birds during April to July. You can enjoy more views as you continue on the worn grassy path, crossing through pasture land. Continue on this path, where you will reach a gate back to the car park.

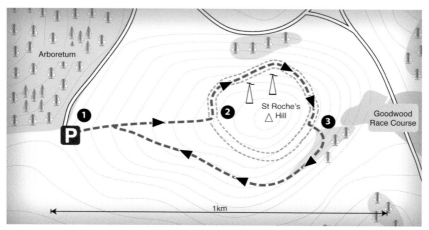

18. Stoughton Down Chall - 3.3 miles - 2hrs 30min

On this circular walk, as you reach Kingley Vale National Nature Reserve, you will pass through what is thought to be one of Europe's most abundant yew tree woodlands. Some of the yew trees are estimated to be over 2,000 years old. There are also mixed deciduous trees amongst the yews and coniferous forest plantations. You will have a gentle but steady climb and on reaching the top there are wonderful views across the beautiful countryside. There are grassland glades and scrub, with some heather on the plateau.

How to get there – From Chichester, take the A286 signed for Lavant and Midhurst. After passing through Lavant look for the left turn onto the B2141, following the brown sign for Uppark. You will pass through the village of Chilgrove and then turn left following the sign for East Marden and West Bourne. On reaching East Marden follow the sign for West Bourne and Stoughton. Continue on this road, where you will reach the car park on your left on a bend in the road.

Grid Reference – SU 814126   **Nearest Postcode** – P018 9JQ

Parking – Free in Forestry Commission car park

Facilities – There are no facilities

You will need – Dog lead, dog bags and water for your dog

The Walk

1 From the car park, take the path which passes beside the metal barrier. Continue on the wide track, with a farm field on your left and beech woodland on your right. Ascend gradually, and after passing the field on your left you will have woodland on each side. Take a wide grassy path on your left, indicated by a finger post, and continue through the woods.

Continue to ascend gradually, and the path will narrow a little after passing a large yew tree on your right. Ignore a path which veers to your right. Pass a finger post on your right and continue straight ahead. On reaching a small field on your left and an avenue of mature beech trees, call your dog close or put him on a lead. There is a house and garden on your left. You are now on an access track, so listen for traffic. There is an arch of beech trees as they join together from both sides of the track.

The track becomes a little steep. **2** As you reach the top of the hill, turn right and follow the sign on the finger post for bridleway. There may be cyclists and horse riders on this track. Continue on the track between the trees, which are mostly hazel coppice. Pass a turning bay for forestry vehicles and continue on the bridleway. There are some yew trees amongst the hazel on your left, and a conifer forest on your right.

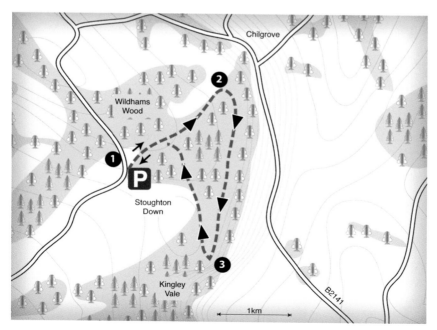

After passing a gate on your left and a finger post, continue straight ahead, where there are now conifer trees on your left and broadleaf trees and conifers on your right. You will enter Kingley Vale National Nature Reserve. Continue straight ahead, passing an interpretation panel on your left. There are mixed broadleaf trees here.

Pass a garden fence on your right and then a gate on your left, where you will reach a finger post. Continue straight ahead, passing through the woodland glade on a wide grassy path. The path splits in two ahead. Take the path on your left and continue, passing another finger post. Stay on the wide grassy track, which is lined with yew trees. There are also ash, hawthorn and oak trees.

Begin to ascend gradually on the path. You will have views on your left, where the trees allow, of woods and fields which stretch out for miles. Pass a glade on your right and continue on the undulating path. There is yew and scrub on both sides of the path.

You will reach another path, a finger post and an interpretation panel. Take a last look at the views here and then turn right. ❸ The path descends between scrub. You will enter dark conifer forest, which will offer shade on a hot day. As you continue to descend, there are beech woods on your right. On leaving the forest you will reach another path. Turn right on this path, now with fields on your left and views across to the woodlands. There are beech woods on your right.

You will reach a series of paths at the end of the field. Take the path straight ahead and to your left, indicated by a finger post and blue arrow. Descend into the beech woods. As you descend, the woodland changes to mixed broadleaf trees. On meeting another path, turn left. Ignore a familiar path on your right and now continue the way you came, descending with woods on your left and a field on your right. You will soon reach the car park.

19. Harting Down

Chall - 3.8 miles - 3hrs 30mins

This circular walk is truly delightful. There are stunning views from the off, as you walk on the flower-rich down. After a hard but fairly short ascent you will reach the top of Beacon Hill, the Iron Age hill fort. You will have wonderful panoramic views from here. You will then descend into an amazing wooded valley after passing scrub, woodland, and colourful meadows, where you will see many butterflies in the summer months. There may be livestock throughout this walk. There are no roads.

How to get there – From Petersfield take the B2146 signed for South Harting. On reaching South Harting, continue on the B2146 following the sign for Emsworth for a short way. On seeing a sign for Chilgrove, turn left onto the B2141. Continue on this road, turning left when you see the brown National Trust sign for Harting Down.

Grid Reference – SU 790180
Nearest Postcode – GU31 5PN

Parking – National Trust, pay by mobile phone.

Facilities – There are no facilities

You will need – Dog leads, dog bags, and water for your dog in hot weather

Countryside Dog Walks - South Downs, Central

The Walk

1 The walk starts near the furthest end of the car park, but before the last parking bay on the bend. Veer right on the worn grassy path, where you will see a gate ahead. Cross the edge of the meadow, with trees on your left.

On reaching the gate and finger post, pass through the small gate and continue straight ahead, keeping your dog under close control as there may be cattle grazing. They are a gentle breed and are used for conservation grazing. You will see another path on your left, which runs parallel to the path, which you are on.

There are wonderful views on your left as you move away from the trees. The path ascends to the brow of a hill. The views expand here. Descend again, through the middle of a flower-rich, hilly meadow. As you get near to the dip, and a line of scrub ahead, take a path on your left. You will almost immediately reach another path, which is the South Downs Way (SDW) long-distance path. Turn right and continue on the stark white chalk path.

The path will descend amongst the trees, where there is a steep bank on your left. On reaching a gate, pass through it, where you will soon reach the dip in the hill. There may be cattle in this field, so keep your dog under close control. Pass a finger post on your left and continue straight ahead, following the sign for Beacon Hill.

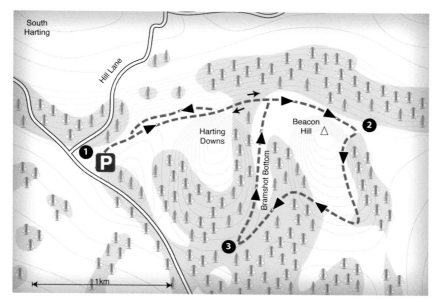

The path, as you will see, becomes quite steep. On nearing the top, pass through a gate, keeping your dog under close control or on a lead as there may be sheep grazing. You will reach a trig point and toposcope, where you are at the highest point of your walk: Beacon Hill, an Iron Age Hill Fort. The views on a clear day are glorious.

Read the direction from the toposcope and head east. You will soon see a finger post near to a belt of trees on your left. Descend the grassy bank, which is quite steep. ❷ Just before reaching the finger post turn right on a track, following beside a stock fence on your left. You are now on the SDW.

Ascend, a little steeply, where you will have stunning views on your left of rolling hills and beautiful broadleaved woodland. On your right you will see the ridged boundary of the Iron Age Hill Fort. The views extend on your left as you continue. You will reach a wood on your left and soon after a finger post. Turn right staying on the SDW, ascending gently.

Continue beside a stock fence on your left, with trees and scrub beyond it. On your right there is open pasture. Pass through a small gate ahead and continue between the stock fence and woodland. You will reach another finger post. Turn left here, leaving the SDW. Descend into a lovely wooded valley. There is gorse scrub and thick hawthorn on both sides of the path, with grassland.

You will eventually reach a finger post. ❸ Turn right and then almost immediately left, just as you pass a ringed split rail fenced enclosure. Pass the enclosed dew pond on your left, keeping dogs away from the water as it is a wildlife pond. Continue through the bottom of the valley, surrounded by wooded slopes.

As the trees close in, you will begin to ascend gently on the path. Continue on this grassy path for some distance. You will ascend out of the valley, and as you near the top you will reach a fork. Take the path, which bends to your left and which is quite steep. On reaching another path turn left, where the path immediately splits in two. Take the path ahead and right, and then almost immediately, turn right on a narrow path. You will reach another path soon after. Turn left on this path to re-join the SDW, where you will again have stunning views.

Ascend to the top of the hill, and you will see a historic ruin just after reaching the trees on your right. As you continue you will see a familiar gate ahead. On reaching the trees take a path on your left and pass through the gate. Cross the meadow to return back to the car park.

20. Durford Wood
Medium - 2.2 miles - 1hr 30min

This is a lovely woodland circular walk, which descends gradually into the wooded valley. There are some stunning sections of woodland, which are mainly oak and silver birch. There are also blocks of conifer plantations. Your dog can enjoy the freedom from livestock, but there may be deer in the area. There are no roads.

How to get there –From Petersfield take the A272 and follow the sign for Midhurst. On reaching a junction continue straight ahead, following the sign for Rake on the B2070. Turn right, following the sign for Rogate, passing the Jolly Drover pub. Continue on this road, where you will reach the car park on your right.

Grid Reference – SU 790259
Nearest Postcode – GU33 7QL

Parking – Free in National Trust car park

Facilities – There are no facilities

You will need – Dog leads, dog bags and water for your dog.

The Walk

❶ From the car park, go through the gate, which is opposite the car park entrance. There is water here on your left if your dog needs a drink. Descend the path on the edge of the woods, with a garden fence on your right and a bank on your left.

At the bottom of the hill you will reach a finger post. **❷** Take the path on your left here, passing the National Trust sign. Continue to descend gently, with pine woods on your left and mixed woodland on your right. Bracken dominates the woodland floor.

There is a path running parallel on your right. The woodland slopes above on your left and below on your right. The path is sandy and rutted in places, and there is a bank on your right. Continue on this path for some distance. You will reach a way-marker on your right. **❸** Take the path on your right here, where you will cross the path which was parallel to the path you were on. Continue straight ahead, ascending on a path through the woods.

You will see pockets of heather and bilberry amongst the bracken. As the path levels out, the woods are dominated by silver birch and oak trees. The path ascends again and you will pass some rhododendron on your right. Scots pine trees dominate the woodland now. On meeting another path, turn left.

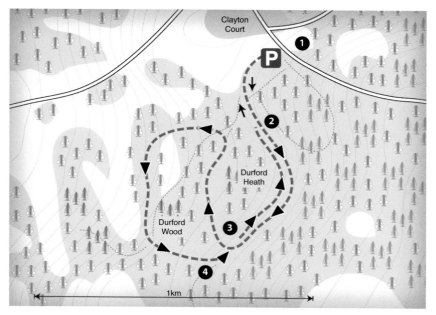

Descend on the path and ignore a path on your left soon after. The woods are mainly oak trees here, with bilberry covering the woodland floor.

You will pass through a clearing, with a house on your far right and views on your left. Enter back into the woods, continue around a left hand bend and then descend. As you continue, bracken will dominate the woodland floor once again. The woods change to a mix of pine, silver birch and oak trees.

❸ On reaching another path turn left, ignoring the path which leads to a gate. The path is sandy again here and you are almost at the bottom of the wooded valley. Ignore a path ahead and to your right, which passes between banks. Continue straight ahead. There is a path parallel on your right.

Continue straight ahead with the bank on your right. You will cross a path, which you previously ascended. Oak trees dominate the woods here on your left. The path will begin to ascend gradually. You will join another path; continue straight ahead here. Just afterwards, you will pass a familiar finger post and path. Continue to ascend on the path to retrace your steps back to the car park.

90

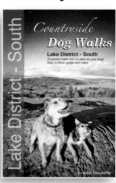
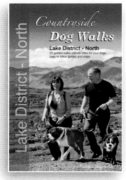
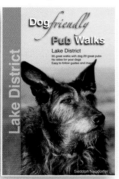

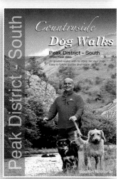
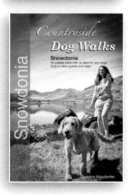

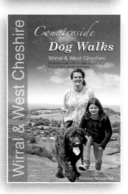